FLOAT AND SINK

by Robin Nelson

Lerner Books • London • New York • Minneapolis

What **floats?**

What **sinks?**

A duck floats.

A rock sinks.

A feather floats.

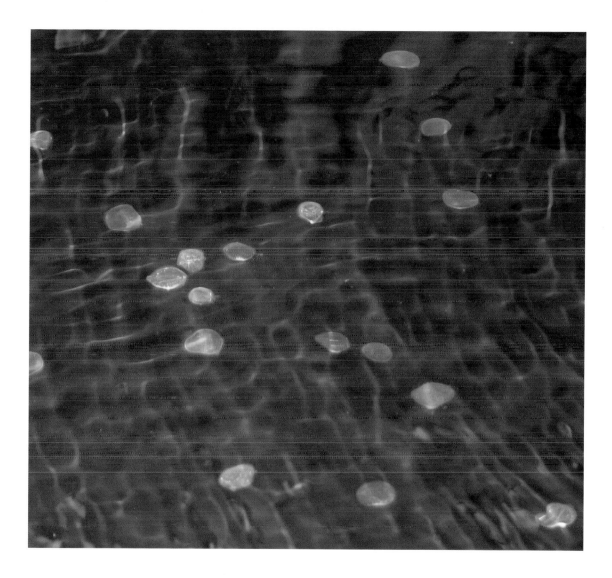

A coin sinks.

A boat floats.

An **anchor** sinks.

A ball floats.

A spoon sinks.

A **fishing float** floats.

A **hook** sinks.

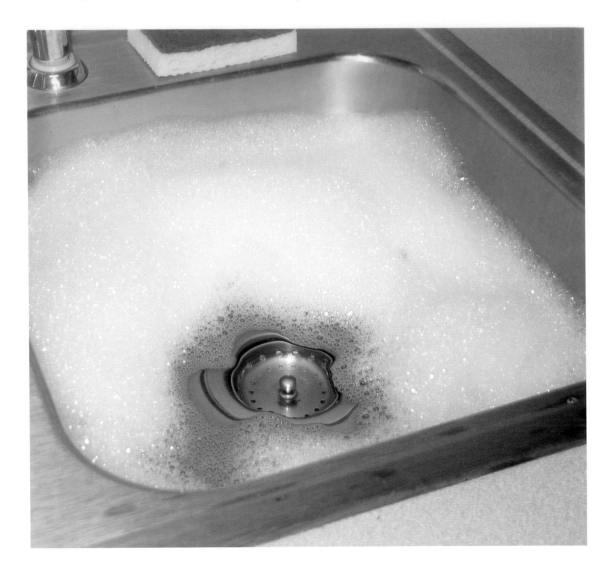

Bubbles float.

Soap sinks.

Can you float?

Can you sink?

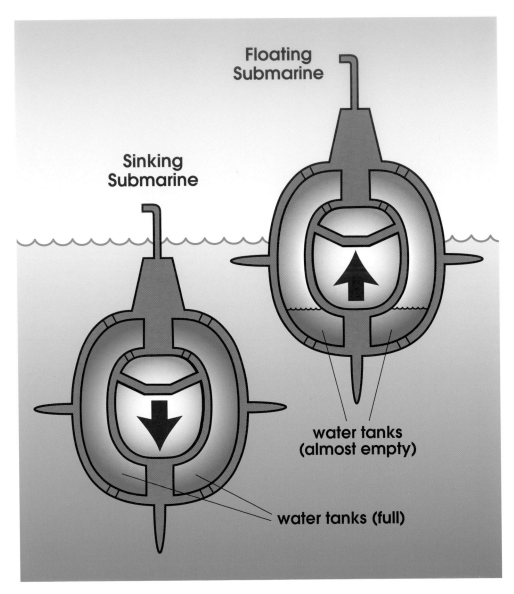

Floating
Submarine

Sinking
Submarine

water tanks
(almost empty)

water tanks (full)

18

How does a submarine sink and float?

Sinking
Submarines have big tanks. The submarine lets water into the tanks. It lets in water until it is heavy enough to sink.

Floating
The submarine pumps the water out into the sea. It gets lighter and rises to the surface. The submarine floats.

Float and Sink Facts

 Gravity makes things sink in water. Gravity is a force that pulls things down.

 An object floats if it is lighter than the water under it. The object floats because the water pushes up against it.

 A small, heavy object will usually sink.

 A large, light object will usually float.

A heavy ship can float because its weight is spread out over a large area. That way, more water is pushing up against the boat to keep it floating.

 It is easier for an object to float in salt water than in fresh water.

An iron ball would take more than an hour to sink to the bottom of the deepest part of the ocean.

Glossary

 anchor – something heavy that keeps a boat in one place

 fishing float – a floating ball or object on a fishing line

 floats – sits on top of water

 hook – a curved piece of metal used to catch fish

 sinks – goes down under the water

Index

The photographs in this book are reproduced through the courtesy of: PhotoDisc Royalty Free by Getty Images, cover, pp. 2, 16, 22 (middle); © Todd Strand/Independent Picture Service, pp. 3, 4, 6, 7, 11, 14, 15, 22 (bottom); © Elwin Trump, p. 5; Stockbyte Royalty Free, p. 8; © Ken Hoppen, pp. 9, 22 (top); Corbis Royalty Free, pp. 10, 13, 17, 22 (second from bottom); © Russell Graves, pp. 12, 22 (second from top).

Illustration on page 18 by Laura Westlund.

This book was first published in the United States of America in 2004.

First published in the United Kingdom in 2008 by
Lerner Books,
Dalton House,
60 Windsor Avenue,
London SW19 2RR

Website address: www.lernerbooks.co.uk

This edition was updated and edited for UK publication by Discovery Books Ltd., Unit 3, 37 Watling Street, Leintwardine, Shropshire SY7 0LW

Words in **bold** are explained in the glossary on page 22.

British Library Cataloguing in Publication Data

Nelson, Robin, 1971-
Float and sink. - (First step nonfiction. Forces)
1. Floating bodies - Juvenile literature 2. Bouyant ascent
(Hydrodynamics) - Juvenile literature
I. Title
532.2'5

ISBN-13: 978 1 58013 366 1

Printed in China